LITERATURE
WORKS

A Collection of Readings

COLLECTION 1/2

Silver Burdett Ginn
A Division of Simon & Schuster
160 Gould Street
Needham Heights, MA 02194

Acknowledgments appear on page 144, which constitutes an extension of this copyright page.

© 1997 Silver Burdett Ginn Inc.

ISBN: 0-663-61217-9   1 2 3 4 5 6 7 8 9 10 RRD 03 02 01 00 99 98 97 96

Literature WORKS

A Collection of Readings

COLLECTION 1/2

THEMES

Animals Everywhere

The World We Share

SILVER BURDETT GINN

Needham, MA   Parsippany, NJ
Atlanta, GA   Deerfield, IL   Irving, TX   Santa Clara, CA

Theme 3 ANIMALS EVERYWHERE

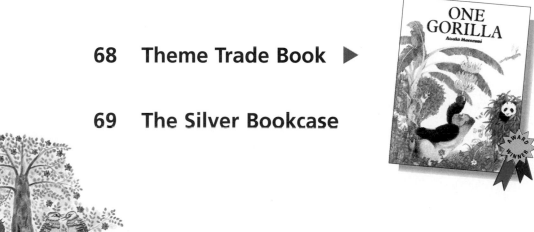

Animals Everywhere

Having a G-r-reat Time in India

KENYA

Greetings from Costa Rica

Keeping Cool in Canada

Theme
3 Contents

Meet Pat Hutchins

Hi! I'm **Pat Hutchins**.

I grew up in a small village in England. Many birds and animals lived in the fields and woods where I played. Later, I made up stories about those animals. One of the stories is **Good-Night, Owl!**

Pat Hutchins

GOOD-NIGHT, OWL!

PAT HUTCHINS

AWARD WINNER

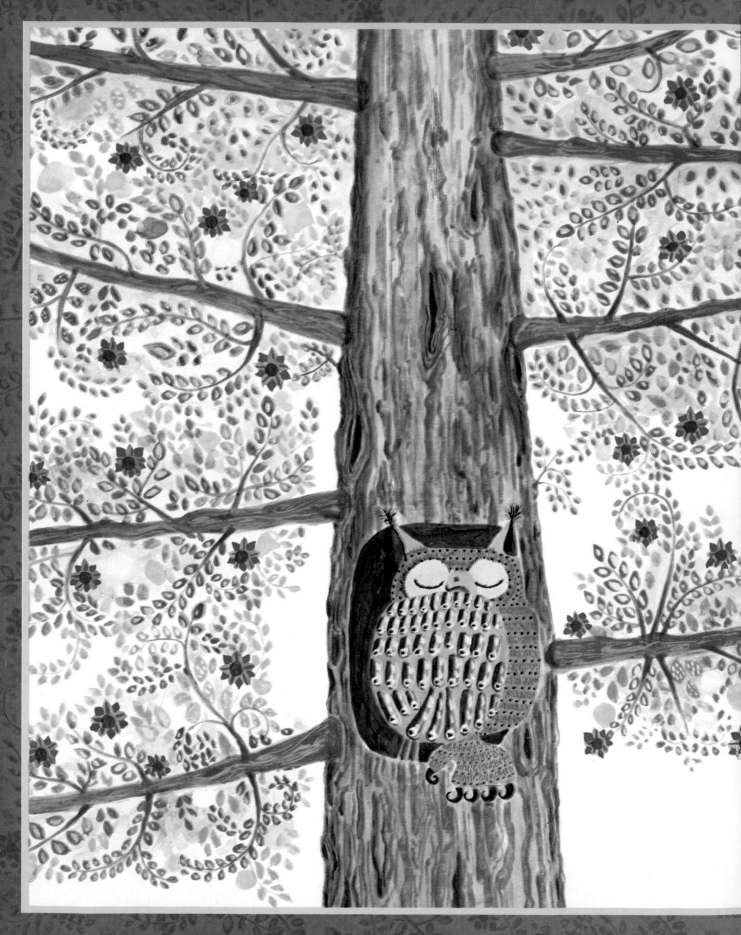

Owl tried to sleep.

The bees buzzed,
buzz buzz,
and Owl tried to sleep.

The squirrel cracked nuts,
crunch crunch,
and Owl tried to sleep.

The crows croaked,
caw caw,
and Owl tried to sleep.

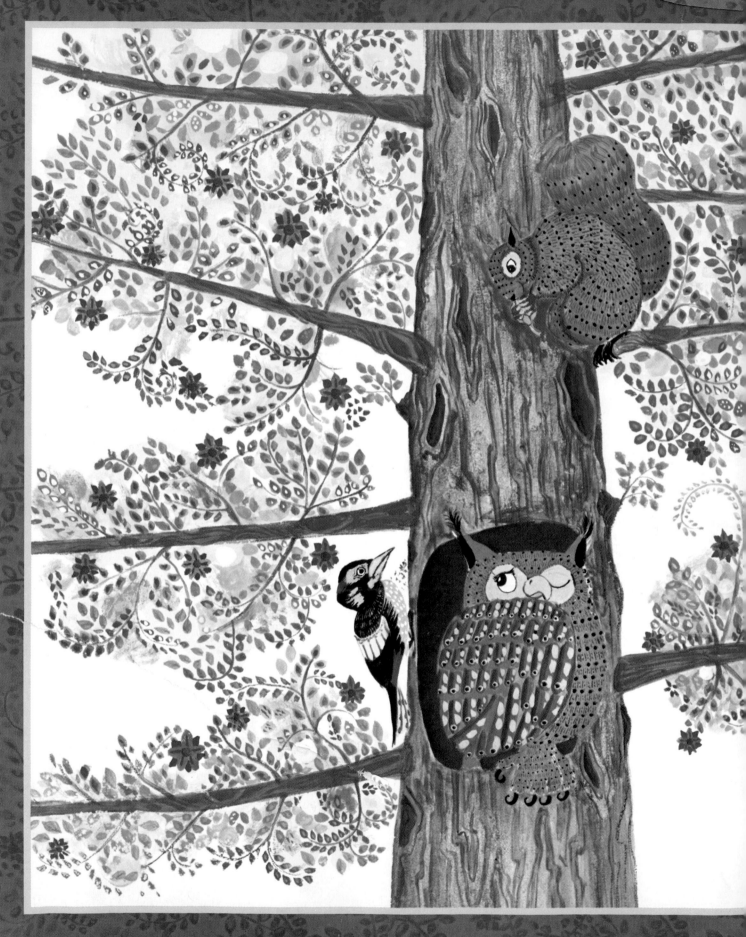

The woodpecker pecked,
rat-a-tat! rat-a-tat!
and Owl tried to sleep.

The starlings chittered,
twit-twit, twit-twit,
and Owl tried to sleep.

The jays screamed,
ark ark,
and Owl tried to sleep.

The cuckoo called,
cuckoo cuckoo,
and Owl tried to sleep.

The robin peeped,
pip pip,
and Owl tried to sleep.

The sparrows chirped,
cheep cheep,
and Owl tried to sleep.

The doves cooed,
croo croo,
and Owl tried to sleep.

The bees buzzed, buzz buzz.
The squirrel cracked nuts,
crunch crunch.
The crows croaked, caw caw.
The woodpecker pecked,
rat-a-tat! rat-a-tat!
The starlings chittered,
twit-twit, twit-twit.
The jays screamed, ark ark.
The cuckoo called,
cuckoo cuckoo.
The robin peeped, pip pip.
The sparrows chirped,
cheep cheep.
The doves cooed, croo croo,
and Owl couldn't sleep.

Then darkness fell
and the moon came up.
And there wasn't a sound.

Owl screeched,
screech screech,
and woke everyone up.

cheep
cheep

pip pip

crunch
crunch

Animals make lots of sounds!

Draw a picture of an animal from the story. Write the sound it makes.

Can you make the sound?

CRUNCH
CRUNCH

BUZZ

BUZZ

Creatures of the Night

Owls

Fireflies

Raccoons

Owls can turn their heads almost all the way around. They have huge eyes to see in the dark.

Fireflies have lights on their bodies. They talk to each other by flashing these lights on and off.

Raccoons hunt for food at night. They use their fingers to swim, climb, and dig.

41

It Is I, the Little Owl

Who is it up there on top of the lodge?
Who is it up there on top of the lodge?
It is I,
The little owl,
coming down—
It is I,
The little owl,
coming down—
coming down—
down—
coming
down—
down—

Who is it whose eyes are shining up there?
Who is it whose eyes are shining up there?
It is I,
The little owl,
coming down—
It is I,
The little owl,
coming down—
coming—
down—
coming
down—
down—

Chippewa Song

Meet Tana Hoban and Her Daughter Miela Ford

Tana Hoban is a photographer. She took the pictures for **Little Elephant**. Tana likes to visit the zoo where Little Elephant lives.

Miela Ford wrote the words for **Little Elephant**. This was Miela's first book. But, Tana has written many books.
They both say they loved making a book together.

LITTLE ELEPHANT

photographs by **TANA HOBAN** story by **MIELA FORD**

AWARD WINNER

I am a little elephant.

This is my mother.

She lets me play in the water.

First one toe, then two.

A big splash.

Lots of bubbles.

Up goes my trunk.

Swing it around.

Under I go.

Can you see me?

Here I am.

Time to get out.

This is hard.

Oops!

Can I make it?

Yes, I can!

Hurry now.

Where is my mother?

Waiting for me!

 IN RESPONSE

Some things are easy for
Little Elephant to do.
Some things are hard.

What is easy or hard
for you to do?

Draw a picture of
one thing you
can do.

It's a Girl!

**The National Zoo
is happy to announce the
birth of a baby elephant!**

**Kumari
was born on
December 14.**

**She weighs 264 pounds
and is 3 feet tall.**

Kumari stays close to her mother.

She is getting a checkup. Everything looks good!

Kumari is playing with a ball and learning to use her trunk.

Theme Trade Book

One Gorilla

by Atsuko Morozumi, Farrar, Straus & Giroux, 1990

Count the animals from one to ten.
Some of them are hard to find.
Can you find them all?

More Books for You to Enjoy

Splash, Splash

by Jeff Sheppard, illustrated by Dennis Panek, Macmillan, 1994

Some animals like the water and some do not. Find out how different animals feel when they fall in a lake.

Farm Noises

by Jane Miller, Simon & Schuster, 1989

Listen to all the sounds you can hear on a farm. What a noisy place it is!

fiddle-i-fee

by Jakki Wood, Bradbury Press, 1994

A boy feeds his animal friends and receives noisy thank-you's from all of them.

The World We Share

Contents

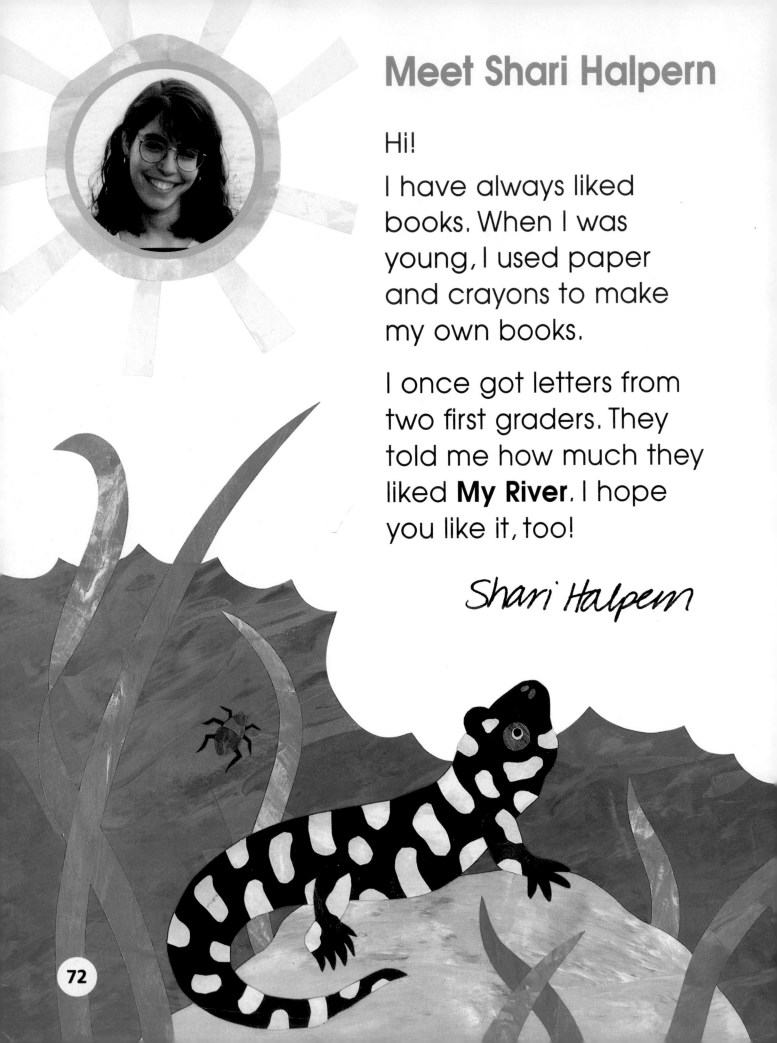

Meet Shari Halpern

Hi!

I have always liked books. When I was young, I used paper and crayons to make my own books.

I once got letters from two first graders. They told me how much they liked **My River**. I hope you like it, too!

Shari Halpern

MY
RIVER
by Shari Halpern

Whose river is this?

It's my river.

It's our river.

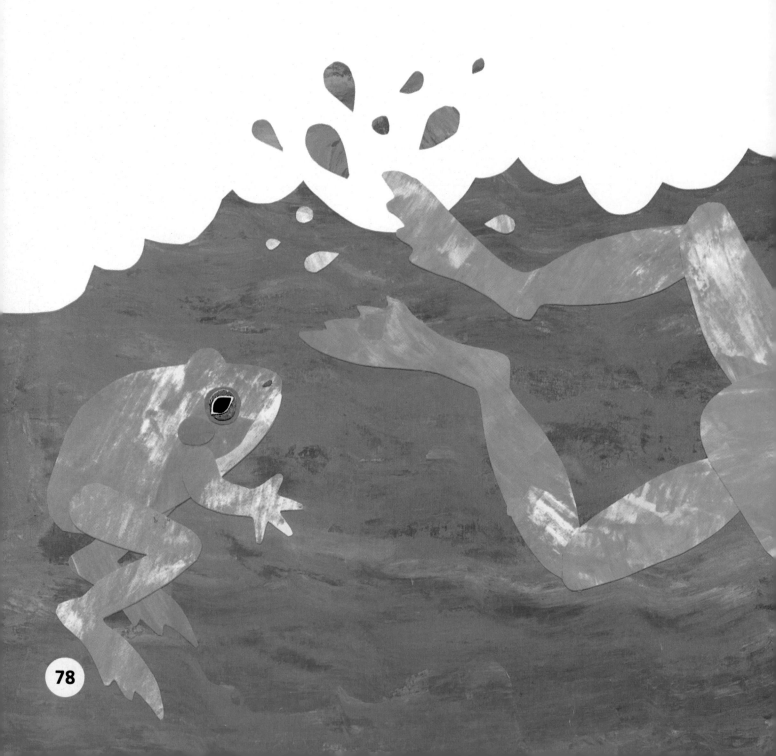

It's everyone's river!

This is my home.

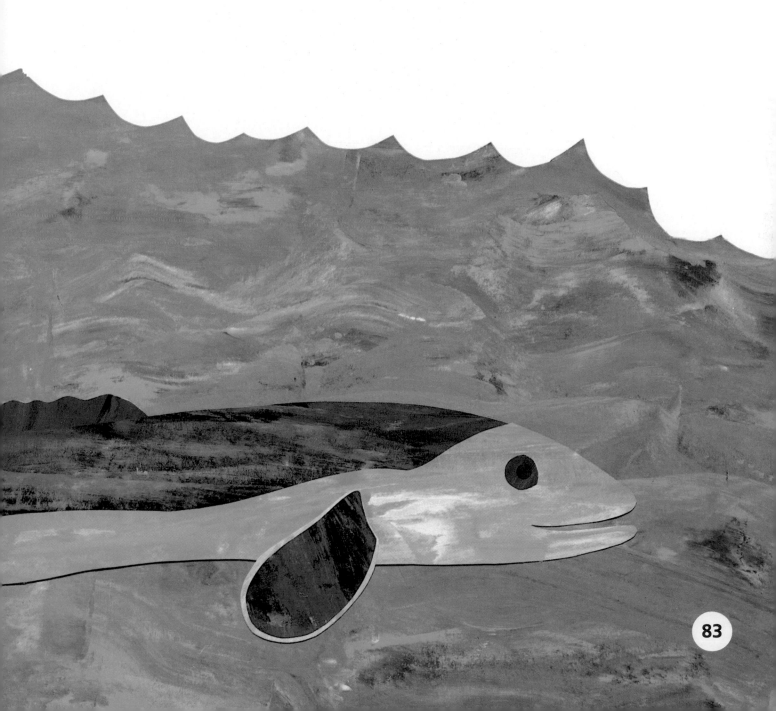

We live here, too.

I was born here.

This is where we grow.

I need the river.

So do we.

We *all* need the river!

This river is mine.

97

Whose river is it?

It's *everyone's* river!

 turtle

 vegetation

 frog

 muskrat

 fish

 water beetle

 eel

 duck

 salamander

 crayfish

 dragonfly

 children

Pretend you are an animal from the story. Draw a picture to show how you need the river.

Write or tell about it.

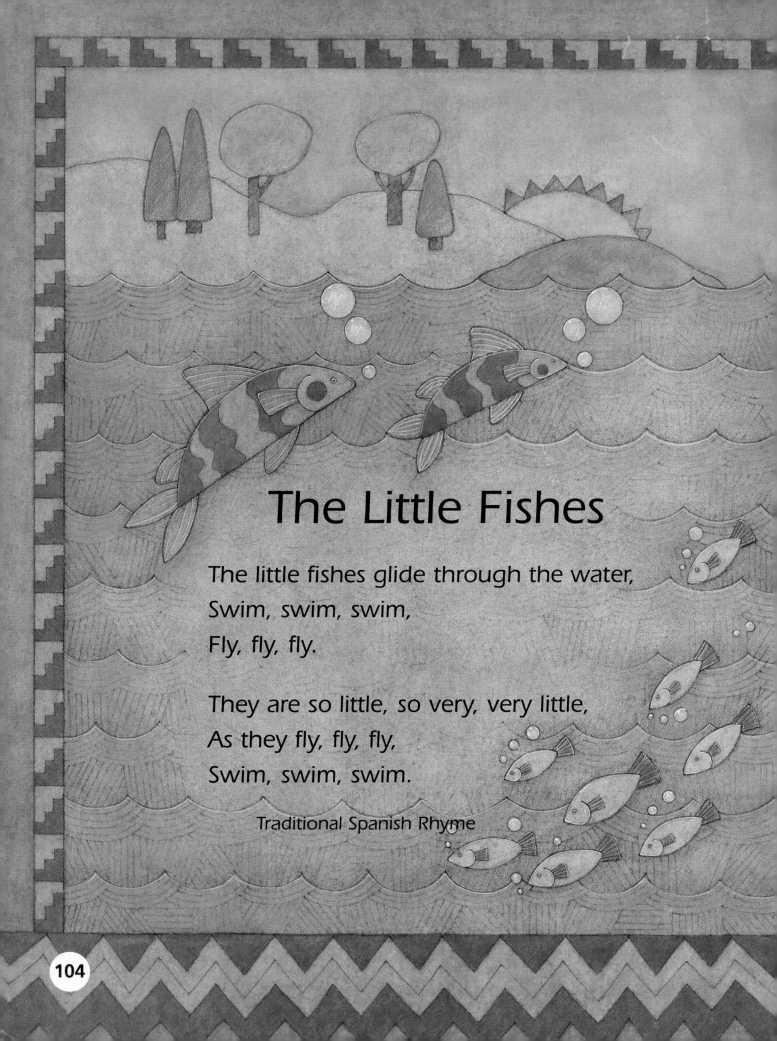

The Little Fishes

The little fishes glide through the water,
Swim, swim, swim,
Fly, fly, fly.

They are so little, so very, very little,
As they fly, fly, fly,
Swim, swim, swim.

Traditional Spanish Rhyme

Los pescaditos

Los pescaditos andan en el agua,
nadan, nadan, nadan,
vuelan, vuelan, vuelan.

Son chiquititos, chiquititos, chiquititos,
vuelan, vuelan, vuelan,
nadan, nadan, nadan.

Meet the Illustrator

Nonny Hogrogian learned about art from her father. On Sundays her father liked to paint pictures. On Mondays he went to work. While he was at work, Nonny added to his pictures. That is how she started to draw.

I AM EYES

NI MACHO

Words by Leila Ward
Pictures by Nonny Hogrogian

The sun wakes me.
I say,
"Ni macho!"
It means, "I am awake."
But it says,
"I am eyes!"

I see sunflowers and skies.

I see grasses and giraffes.

I see stars and starlings.

I see elands and elephants.

I see crabs and coral.

I see sun and sand.

I see the moon and moonflowers.

I see donkeys and monkeys.

I see coconuts and camels.

I see kites and Kilimanjaro.

I see flowers and flamingos.

I see pineapples and pelicans.

And everywhere
where I am eyes, I see butterflies.

What did the little girl in the story see? Imagine the little girl comes to your home.

Draw something you would show her. Write about it.

Where in the World Is Kenya?

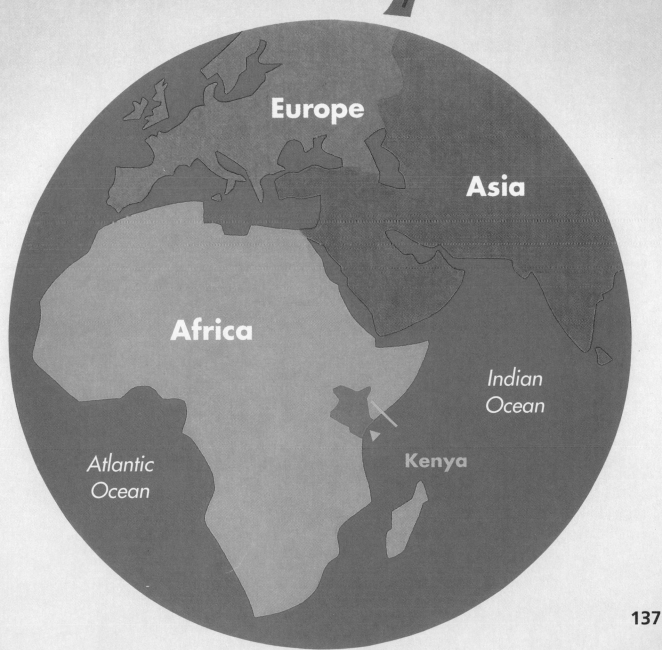

What Can You See in Kenya?

by Veronica Freeman Ellis

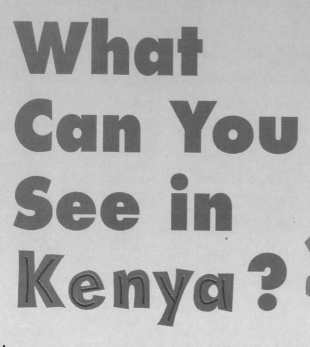

Exciting animals live in Kenya! Some are cheetahs, giraffes, and zebras. Cheetahs are the fastest land animals in the world. ▼

◀ Nairobi, Kenya's capital, is a big city. It has nice parks and lots of tall buildings.

There are large outdoor markets in cities like Nairobi. Food, clothes, and things for the home are sold there. ▶

◀ In Kenya many things are homemade. People weave colorful baskets.

AFRICAN ART

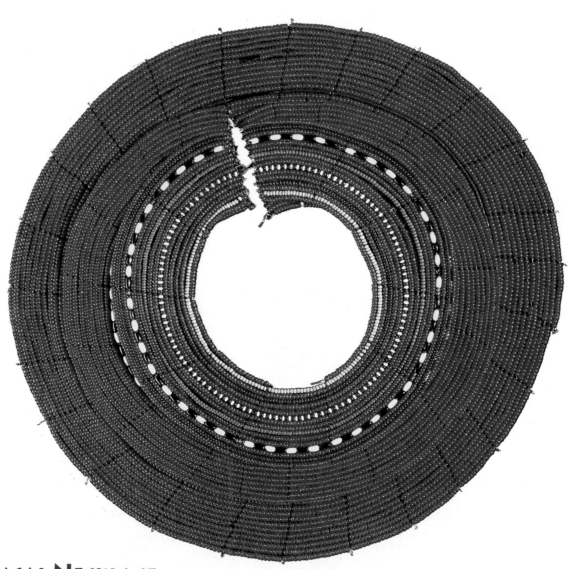

MASAI NECKLACE
Tanzania, late 1900's

ELEPHANT MASK
Cameroon, late 1800's

SCULPTURE OF
AN ONI (KING)
Nigeria, late 1400's

Theme Trade Book

Citybook

by Shelley Rotner and
Ken Kreisler, Orchard Books, 1994

Kevin visits the city and discovers it is a
fun place to be.

More Books for You to Enjoy

Rosie's Walk

by Pat Hutchins, Collier's Books, 1968

Will the fox be able to catch Rosie the hen?

Does a Mouse Have a House?

by Anne Miranda, Bradbury Press, 1994

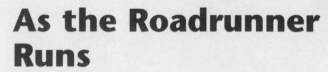

Other animals have homes, but what about the mouse? Turn the pages and find out.

As the Roadrunner Runs

by Gail Hartman, illustrated by Cathy Bobak, Bradbury Press, 1994

Follow the paths of a lizard, jackrabbit, roadrunner, and others. Have more fun with maps!

143

ACKNOWLEDGMENTS

Grateful acknowledgment is made to the following publishers, authors, and agents for their permission to reprint copyrighted material. Every effort has been made to locate all copyright proprietors; any errors or omissions in copyright notice are inadvertent and will be corrected in future printings as they are discovered.

"Creatures of the Night" from **Night Creatures** by Susanne Santoro Whayne, illustrated by Steven Schindler. Illustrations ©1993 by Steven Schindler. Used by permission of the publisher, Simon & Schuster Books for Young Readers.

Good-Night, Owl! by Pat Hutchins. Copyright ©1972 by Pat Hutchins. Reprinted with permission of the American publisher, Macmillan Books for Young Readers, Simon & Schuster Children's Publishing Division, and of the British publisher, The Bodley Head, a division of Random House UK Limited.

I Am Eyes*Ni Macho by Leila Nash Ward. Illustrated by Nonny Hogrogian. Text copyright ©1978 by Leila Nash Ward. Illustrations copyright ©1978 by Nonny H. Kherdian. Reprinted by permission of Greenwillow Books, a division of William Morrow & Company, Inc.

"It is I, the Little Owl" from **Songs of the Chippewa** edited by John Bierhorst. Copyright © 1974 by John Bierhorst. Reprinted by permission of the author.

Little Elephant by Miela Ford. Photographs by Tana Hoban. Text copyright ©1994 by Miela Ford. Photographs copyright ©1994 by Tana Hoban. Reprinted by permission of Greenwillow Books, a division of William Morrow & Company, Inc.

My River by Shari Halpern. Copyright ©1992 by Shari Halpern. Reprinted with permission of Macmillan Books for Young Readers, Simon & Schuster Children's Publishing Division.

Phonetic respelling system from **The World Book Encyclopedia.** ©1995 World Book, Inc. By permission of the publisher.

COVER: Cover photography ©1996 by Jade Albert Studio. Cover illustration ©1996 by Delana Bettoli. Cover design, art direction and production by Design Five.

ILLUSTRATION: **42–43**, Shonto Begay; **66–67**, Cyndy Patrick; **72–73**, Shari Halpern; **104–105**, Kat Thacker; **137–138**, Zita Asbaghi.

PHOTOGRAPHY: Unless otherwise indicated, photographs of book covers and of children's art were provided by Ulsaker Studio, Inc. Background photograph for Silver Bookcase by Allan Penn for SBG. Credits listed below for children's art indicate the name of the artist. The abbreviation SBG stands for Silver Burdett Ginn. **8**, (t.l.) © Gerard Lacz/Peter Arnold, Inc., (t.r.) © James Carmichael/The Image Bank, (b.l.) John Serafin, (b.r.) © 1994 Joseph Van Os/The Image Bank; **9**, (t.l.) © Cralle 1993/The Image Bank, (t.r.) © S. Vidler/Superstock; **10**, courtesy Greenwillow Books; **10–11**, Lou Goodman for SBG; **40**, Doug Mindell for SBG, drawings by Nicholas Morley; **44**, courtesy Miela Ford; **44–45**, Lou Goodman for SBG; **66–67**, Lou Goodman for SBG; **67**, (all) National Zoological Park, Smithsonian Institution, photo by Jessie Cohen; **72**, courtesy Shari Halpern; **106**, courtesy Nonny Hogrogian; **136**, drawing by Janna Savage; **138**, (b.) © SBG, photo by John Serafin; **139**, (t.l.) © H. Kanus/Superstock, (t.r.) © Glenn Oliver/Visuals Unlimited, (b.) © Robert Frerck/Odyssey Productions; **140**, photograph by Franko Khoury, National Museum of African Art, Eliot Elisofon Archives, Smithsonian Institution; **141**, (l.) Upper Half of a Figure of an Oni, Museum of Ife Antiquities, Nigeria, photo © Dirk Bakker 1980/photography by Dirk Bakker, (r.) Elephant mask, Western Grassfields, Cameroon, wood, h. 43 in., private collection, courtesy of Allan Stone Gallery, photograph by Jerry L. Thompson, courtesy of The Museum for African Art, New York.